J 530.8 CAT
Cato, Sheila, 1936-
Measuring /

A Question of Math Book

Measuring

by Sheila Cato
illustrations by Sami Sweeten

SANTA FE SPRINGS CITY LIBRARY
11700 E. TELEGRAPH RD.
SANTA FE SPRINGS, CA 90670
(562) 868-7738

Carolrhoda Books, Inc./Minneapolis

This edition published in 1999 by Carolrhoda Books, Inc.

Copyright © 1998 by Brown Packaging Partworks Limited.

All rights to this edition reserved. No part of this book may be reproduced, stored in a retrieval system, or transmitted in any form or by any means, electronic, mechanical, photocopying, recording, or otherwise, without the prior permission of Carolrhoda Books, Inc., except for the inclusion of brief quotations in an acknowledged review.

Carolrhoda Books, Inc., c/o The Lerner Publishing Group
241 First Avenue North, Minneapolis, MN 55401 U.S.A.

Website address: www. lernerbooks.com

LIBRARY OF CONGRESS CATALOGING-IN-PUBLICATION DATA
Cato, Sheila
    Measuring / by Sheila Cato : illustrations by Sami Sweeten.
        p.   cm. — (A question of math book)
    Summary: A group of children demonstrate how to measure weight, fluids, distance, size, and time.
    ISBN 1-57505-323-3 (alk. paper)
    1. Mensuration—Juvenile literature.   [1. Measurement.]
    I. Sweeten, Sami, ill. II. Title. III. Series: Cato, Sheila, 1936-
    Question of math book.
    QA465
    .C24 1999
    530.8—dc21   98-16123

The series A Question of Math is produced by Carolrhoda Books, Inc., in cooperation with Brown Packaging Partworks Limited, London, England. The series is based on a concept by Sidney Rosen, Ph.D.
Series consultant: Kimi Hosoume, University of California at Berkeley
Editor: Anne O'Daly
Designers: Janelle Barker and Duncan Brown

Printed in Singapore
Bound in the United States of America

1 2 3 4 5 6 - JR - 04 03 02 01 00 99

This is Mia. Mia is having fun learning how to measure different things. Her number friend, Digit, is here to help. Take a look at Digit. He is made of numbers. Which numbers can you see?

You can join in the fun, too. If you want to try the activities you will need a balance, a set of kitchen scales, a bathroom scale, different size cups, and a tape measure.

Popcorn has 2 puppies. How can I use the balance to find which puppy is heavier?

It's easy to use a balance, Mia. Put 1 puppy on each side of the balance and watch what happens.

The pan that goes down holds the heavier puppy. Just to be sure, swap the puppies on the balance pans and see which pan goes down this time.

The same puppy is on the lower pan both times so that is the heavier puppy.

Using a Balance

A balance won't tell you how much things weigh, but it shows you which is the heavier of two things.

Now You Try

Find two of your toys and use a balance to see which is heavier. Try to guess which it will be before you start.

Brad and I have bought a bag of our favorite candy. We want to know how much it weighs. What should we use, Digit?

When we weigh small things, we can use scales that are divided into pounds and ounces. You could use a kitchen scale to weigh the bag of candy, Mia.

We use a kitchen scale to measure small amounts of food, especially when we are weighing ingredients for a recipe.

This kitchen scale can weigh objects up to 8 pounds. The space between each pound is divided into 8 equal parts. Each small space measures 2 ounces. Do you know how many ounces there are in one pound, Mia?

There are 16 ounces in 1 pound.
Our bag of candy weighs 10 ounces.

Now You Try

The candy that Mia and Brad bought weighed 10 ounces. If they share the candy so that they both get the same amount, how many ounces would they each have?

Luis and I want to know which of us is heavier. Could you please explain, Digit, how we can find out?

Of course, Mia. You and Luis are much bigger than Popcorn's puppies, so you can't use the balance. A seesaw can help you guess who is heavier, because it will be easier for the heavier person to stay at the bottom on the seesaw. But if you want to know for sure, you need to use a bathroom scale.

Each would have 5 ounces of candy

Bathroom Scale

When we want to weigh heavier things than candy or items of food, we use a bathroom scale.

Bathroom scales weigh things in pounds. When you stand on a scale, the pointer shows you how much you weigh. If you and Luis stand on the scale, one at a time, you can find out how heavy you are.

The pointer stops at 60 when I'm on the scale, so I weigh 60 pounds. And the pointer shows 75 when Luis gets on, so that's 75 pounds. Luis is heavier than I am.

9

Now You Try

How many pounds heavier is Luis than Mia?

Luis is 15 pounds heavier than Mia

Josh, Holly, and I have brought different sized cups to the picnic. We have one bottle of soda to share. How can we share the soda so that we each get the same amount?

Start by filling the smallest cup with soda and pouring it into the largest cup. This one is for Holly.

10

Fill the smallest cup again and pour it into the middle size cup. This one is for Josh. What will you do next, Mia?

That's simple, Digit. I'll fill the smallest cup again for me and then we'll all have the same amount of soda. Although we don't know how much we have, we have shared the bottle of soda equally.

One Way to Measure

Sometimes we use an ordinary container like a cup or glass to measure equal amounts of liquid into other containers.

Now You Try

Use different sized cups and find which one holds the most by pouring water from the smallest into each of the others in turn.

I need 2 quarts of water to make soup for our camp supper. But I only have a 5-quart jug and a 3-quart jug. What should I do, Digit?

We can soon solve that problem, Mia. You know that 5 - 3 = 2, so start by filling the 5-quart jug with water. That's more water than you need. What could you do so that you have only 2 quarts left in the jug?

If I filled the 3-quart jug from the 5-quart jug that would leave 2 quarts in the bigger jug. That's a good way to measure out the right amount of water. Now I can make the soup for supper.

Ounces and Quarts

Liquids are measured in fluid ounces and quarts. There are 32 fluid ounces in 1 quart.

Now You Try

How could Mia measure 7 quarts of water using the two jugs?

Measure 2 quarts as before. Fill the 5-quart jug and add them together. You will have 7 quarts of water.

Holly and I are making an orange drink for the children at our Thanksgiving Dinner. The instructions say "1 part orange juice to 3 parts sparkling water." How should we measure this, Digit?

Let's use a ½-quart jug and start by filling it with orange juice. Now empty this into a large container. Then refill the jug with sparkling water, and add it to the orange juice. What should you do next, Mia?

14

Making a Mixture

Many drinks can be made from a mixture of liquids. It's important to read the instructions carefully when you make a mixture so that you get the right amount.

I'll fill the ½-quart jug again with sparkling water and add it to the mixture. Then I'll do the same once more and the drink will be ready.

Now You Try

How much orange drink did Mia and Holly make for the Thanksgiving Dinner?

Brad and I are measuring our hand spans. First we held our hands against each other to see whose hand is bigger. Now we are going to measure our hands using a ruler. Would you please explain what the numbers on a ruler mean, Digit?

Your ruler is 12 inches long, Mia, so the numbers 0 to 12 show you the length in inches.

They made 2 quarts of drink

16

Using a Ruler

When you measure something using a ruler, remember to start measuring from the left-hand side of the ruler. Make sure you aren't holding it the wrong way up!

Each inch is marked on your ruler with a line. An inch is divided into 16 equal parts. These are marked with smaller lines. If you hold your hands against the ruler, you can measure your hand spans accurately. Remember to put your thumb on the left end of the ruler.

My hand span is exactly 4 inches and Brad's is 5 inches. Brad's hand is bigger than mine.

Now You Try

How much bigger is Brad's hand span than Mia's?

Holly and I are the same age, but she is taller than me. How could we find out how much taller she is?

The best way to do this is to stand against a wall and put a book on your head so that it makes a right angle with the wall. Now make a small mark on the wall with a pencil where the book touches it. Remember to take your shoes off first!

Brad's hand span is 1 inch bigger than Mia's

Measuring Heights

Measuring the difference in height of Mia and Holly doesn't tell you how tall they are. You have to measure the distance from the ground to the marks on the wall to find their heights.

Now find Holly's height using the same method. There are now two marks on the wall. What will you do next, Mia?

If I measure the distance between the two marks with a ruler, that will tell us how much taller Holly is than me.

Now You Try

If Mia is 50 inches tall and Holly is 53 inches, how much taller is Holly?

Holly is 3 inches taller than Mia

Josh, Holly, Luis, and I have bought a bar of chocolate. The chocolate bar is 12 inches long. How can we share it equally between us, and how long would each piece be?

There are four of you sharing the bar of chocolate, so first of all break it in half to get 2 equal pieces.

Now break each of the 2 pieces in half to get 4 pieces all the same length. What will be the length of each piece?

When we break 12 inches in half, each piece will be 6 inches long. When we halve these pieces, we will each have a 3-inch piece of chocolate.

Equal Lengths

When we divide something into equal parts, each part will be the same length and the same weight.

Now You Try

If the children shared a bar of candy 20 inches long, how long would each piece be?

I want to make my room look prettier by putting some ribbon around the frame of my mirror. How much ribbon will I need, Digit?

First of all, Mia, you must measure each side of the mirror.

Each piece of candy is 5 inches long

When you have measured the 4 sides of the mirror, add all the lengths together.
That will tell you how much ribbon you need.

The two long sides of the mirror are both 10 inches. The short sides are both 5 inches.

$$10 \; + \; 10 \; +$$
$$5 \; + \; 5 \; = \; 30$$

I need a piece of ribbon that is 30 inches long.

Adding Lengths

When you measure around an object you can add the lengths together just as you would add numbers.

Now You Try

Use Mia's method to decorate your own mirror, desk, or bookcase. How much ribbon will you need?

We're running in a 15-yard race on sports day. What is the best way to mark the track?

You used a tape measure to measure around your mirror, but you will need a special long tape measure to measure the track.

Tape Measures

Tape measures come in several different lengths. Some are only 36 inches, while others can measure 10 feet or more.

Now You Try

Use a tape measure to find the size of your bedroom, the length of your bed, and some of the furniture. Perhaps you could draw a picture of your room and write the lengths of things on the picture.

This kind of tape measure is divided into inches, feet, and yards. There are 12 inches in a foot and 3 feet in a yard. Put the 0 mark on the start of the track and unwind the tape until you see the number 15.
This is where the track will end.

That looks like a long way to run!

25

When I tell time, I get mixed up between the hour and the half-hour. Could you please explain the difference, Digit.

It can be confusing, Mia. You can always tell by looking at the big hand first.
If it is pointing to 12, it is on the hour, and the small hand will be pointing to a number.

When the big hand is on 6, the small hand is halfway between two numbers.
It's half, or 30 minutes, past the number that the small hand has just passed.

Clock Face

A clock face has the numbers 1 to 12 evenly spaced around the face. It takes 60 minutes or 1 hour for the small hand to move from one number to the next.

Now You Try

What time is it when the big hand is on 6 and the small hand is halfway between 2 and 3?

Our swimming lesson starts at 12:00 and finishes at 12:45.
How long does our lesson last?

You know that there are 60 minutes in one hour, Mia, and it takes 5 minutes for the big hand to move from one number to the next.

The time is 2:30

28

When the big hand is on 3, it's a quarter past the hour that the small hand has just passed. When the big hand is on 9, it's a quarter to the hour that the small hand is coming up to.

Every time the big hand reaches a number, 5 minutes have passed. If your lesson starts at 12:00 and ends at 12:45, how long do you think it lasts?

Our lesson lasts for 45 minutes. If I keep checking the clock, I can make sure I get out of the water on time.

Now You Try

Mia's piano lesson starts at 3:00 and finishes at 3:15. How long does her lesson last?

Josh and I each have $1 to spend and we want to know what we can buy with it. Could you help us please, Digit?

Of course, Mia. You need to know first of all that there are 100 cents in a dollar. Whatever you buy must not add up to more than 100 cents.

30

I need some new pencils. They cost 10 cents each, so 3 pencils will cost 30 cents.
 This toy costs 50 cents. So I have spent 30 + 50 = 80 cents. I have 20 cents left over. That's just enough to buy a piece of candy!

Measuring Money

We use money all the time to pay for things we buy. Money is another way of measuring. But money measures how much something costs, not how long it is or how heavy it is.

Now I know how to find out how much something weighs and how long something is. I know when to use a kitchen scale and when to use a bathroom scale. I know about rulers and tape measures. I can make mixtures and I can measure volumes. I can measure time and I know how much money I have to spend!

Here are some useful measuring words

Length: Length tells you how long something is. It is measured in inches, feet, and yards. There are 12 inches in a foot. There are 3 feet in a yard.

Money: Money is a way of measuring how much something costs. Money is measured in cents, nickels, dimes, quarters, and dollars. There are 100 cents in a dollar. A nickel is 5 cents, a dime is 10 cents, and a quarter is 25 cents.

Time: Time is measured in seconds, minutes, and hours. There are 60 seconds in a minute and 60 minutes in an hour.

Volume: Volume tells you how much space something fills. It is measured in fluid ounces.

Weight: The weight of something tells you how heavy it is. Weight is measured in ounces and pounds.